BRAINPEOPLE

José Rivera

BROADWAY PLAY PUBLISHING INC
New York
www.broadwayplaypublishing.com
info@broadwayplaypublishing.com

BRAINPEOPLE
© Copyright 2019 José Rivera

Cover graphic design by Amelia Nardinelli, American Conservatory Theater

First published by B P P I in December 2008
This edition, revised: June 2019
I S B N: 978-0-88145-832-9

Book design: Marie Donovan
Page make-up: Adobe InDesign
Typeface: Palatino

BRAINPEOPLE was commissioned by South Coast Repertory Theater (Martin Benson and David Emmes, Artistic Directors).

BRAINPEOPLE received its world premiere at the American Conservatory Theater, San Francisco (Carey Perloff, Artistic Director; Heather Kitchen, Executive Director), on 2 February 2008.The cast and creative contributors were as follows:

MAYANNAH .... Lucia Brawley
ANI/LAYNA ...,...Sona Tatoyan
ROSEMARY.. Rene Augesen

Director... Chay Yew
Scenic designer... Daniel Ostling
Costume designer...Lydia Tanji
Lighting designer .... Paul Whitaker
Sound designer... Cliff Caruthers
Casting directors........ Greg Hubbard & Meryl Lind Shaw
Dramaturg .... Michael Paller
Stage manager..June Palladino
Production assistant .... Laura Osborn
Assistant to the Director............................Bruce Coughran

BRAINPEOPLE was made possible by the generous support of the William and Flora Hewlett Foundation for New Works, an endowment fund of The Next Generation Campaign.

Special thanks to Erica Gould, Rebecca Wisocky, Mozhan Marno, Jessica Boucher, Jennifer Blevins, Robert Clyde, Avery Clyde, the Mark Taper Forum Mentor Playwrights, Lisa Peterson, Marissa Chibas, Svetlana Efremova, Jessica Hecht, Jacqueline Kim, Ana Ortiz, Michi Barrall, Juliette Carrillo, Sandra Oh, Morgan Jenness, Len Berkman, Jerry Patch, The Black Dahlia Theatre, Scott Horstein, Nick Mangano, The Garson Theatre, Madeline Brown, Lindsey Marlin, Desi Moreno-Penson, Zenda Tatoyan, Hartford Stage Company, Playwrights Horizons, Tim Sanford, Jeremy Cohen, Lisa Timmel, The Joseph Papp Public Theatre, Johanna Pfaelzer, Karina Arroyave, Zabrina Guevara, Camilia Sanes, Alyssa Bresnahan, Primary Stages, David Lee Strasberg, Carlos San Miguel, Juan Carlos Malpeli, Benoit Beauchamp, Sidney Miller, Vahe Berberian, Lyon Forrest Hill, Jennifer Mae Stevens, Karin Tatoyan, Javi Mulero, Lina Patel, Ariane N Picari, Leah Roy, and Cindy Gendrich.

CHARACTERS & SETTING

MAYANNAH
ROSEMARY
LAYNA

MAYANNAH's *apartment, Los Angeles*
Time: the present.

There is no intermission.

When you sleep in the exile's bed linen or drink from his cup do you know his body or his name? Is there no shame in owning our things?

Three Apples Fell from Heaven, **Micheline Aharonian Marcom**

I felt a Cleaving in my Mind—
As if my Brain has split—
I tried to match it— Seam by Seam—
But could not make them fit.

The thought behind I strove to join
Unto the thought before—
But sequence raveled out of Sound
Like Balls—upon a Floor.

Emily Dickinson

A tiger comes to mind. The twilight here
Exalts the vast and busy Library
And seems to set the bookshelves back in gloom;
Innocent, ruthless, bloodstained, sleek
It wanders through its forest and its day
Printing a track along the muddy banks
Of sluggish streams whose names it does not know
(In its world there are no names or past
Or time to come, only the vivid now)
And makes its way across wild distances
Sniffing the braided labyrinths of smells
And in the wind picking the smell of dawn
And tantalizing scent of grazing deer;
Among the bamboo's slanting stripes I glimpse
The tiger's stripes and sense the bony frame
Under the splendid, quivering cover of skin.
Curving the oceans and the planet's wastes keep us
Apart in vain; from here in a house fall off
In South America I dream of you,
Track you, O tiger of the Ganges' banks.

Jorge Luis Borges

(A once-luxurious penthouse apartment in downtown Los Angeles. The sun sets, forcing the sky into strange colors.)

(Sparkling city lights appear—until the view outside feels like an urban dreamscape as removed from crime, fear, distress as possible.)

(There are big windows; exposed brick; morbid artwork; folkloric, graphic crucifixes; naked statues of Jesus; old books, faded furniture, a once-fancy fireplace with missing tiles, distressed wooden floor.)

(A long, empty table covered in a colorful tablecloth decorated with images of the ancient Taino Indians.)

(Everything was once brightly colored, vibrant, now muted and decayed—as if the room were stuck in time.)

(By the table is ROSEMARY/ROSIE, *early 30s, graceful, slender, beautiful but hungry and worn down by life's tragedies and insults.)*

(Her clothes, shoes and costume jewelry are from the Salvation Army. Her over-done make-up is trashy. She speaks in an Irish accent to an off-stage person.)

ROSEMARY/ROSIE: God, I haven't had meat in so long. I forgot how much I loved the smell!

*(*MAYANNAH *enters from the kitchen with a fancy bowl of melted butter.)*

(She is 30s, an aristocratic Puerto Rican with long dark hair, dark, intense eyes; her clothes are elegant and black; she wears diamond necklaces, earrings, and bracelets.)

MAYANNAH: This butter was made from the milk of cows born and raised in my parents' hometown in Puerto Rico.

ROSEMARY/ROSIE: Red meat, blood, and butter! Wow!

MAYANNAH: Every year I get it flown from the island on a private jet just for this meal.

ROSEMARY/ROSIE: I love that pretty necklace. So glittery.

MAYANNAH: My mother left it for me.

ROSEMARY/ROSIE: And it's absolutely incredible, this place, Mayannah.

(MAYANNAH *pours rum.)*

MAYANNAH: Comes with the best Puerto Rican rum in the world. My family's own label!

ROSEMARY/ROSIE: Like a big, bloody church. All the pretty Jesuses!

MAYANNAH: I collect them. From all over the world.

ROSEMARY/ROSIE: Why are they all naked?

(The doorbell rings.)

MAYANNAH: Ay! That must be her! The other one! I thought she'd never show!

(MAYANNAH *goes off.* ROSEMARY/ROSIE *hungrily stares at the butter.)*

LAYNA: *(Off)* Hello? It's, it's Layna. I'm here. In one piece thank God!

MAYANNAH: *(Off)* Yes! So glad you're here, Layna!

(ROSEMARY/ROSIE *sticks her finger in the butter and tastes it.)*

ROSEMARY/ROSIE: Oh good God, that's bloody fuckin' fab…!

(ROSEMARY/ROSIE *hungrily drinks the butter and licks the bowl.*)

LAYNA: *(Off)* Your home, Mayannah—so dark—but beautiful!

MAYANNAH: *(Off)* You are beautiful! I had no idea!

(MAYANNAH *and* LAYNA, *30s, enter.* LAYNA *is a bookish, obsessive, lovelorn Greek-American woman with piercing eyes beneath glasses. Hair in a ponytail)*

(Though articulate and well-dressed there's something awkward about her: she has a hard time navigating real and emotional space.)

LAYNA: Yeah, well, last time you saw me, I looked like death. Oh, someone's already here. Hi.

MAYANNAH: Layna—meet Rosemary.

ROSEMARY/ROSIE: God, don't call me that awful name. She was not fucking bloody invited! It's Rosie.

MAYANNAH: Oh, I meant—Rosie…

LAYNA: Nice to meet you, Rosie

ROSEMARY/ROSIE: Yeah, okay.

LAYNA: I brought some wine. I don't actually know anything about wine but I read in a pretty good wine magazine that this is a pretty good bottle of wine.

MAYANNAH: Thank you so much, that's so thoughtful.

ROSEMARY/ROSIE: Wine mag? Lame!

LAYNA: So they—they put up these new checkpoints on the 10. God, those soldiers are the dumbest, most Neolithic men in America! They asked for my I D and it took forever. Lucky that your driver had all that cash. Or else I never would have gotten here.

MAYANNAH: Well, you're here with friends now and everything's going to be magic.

LAYNA: Magic? Is that a good thing?

MAYANNAH: Oh, you two: lovely eyes, lovely hands. And we're all really here—in my house—the three of us.

ROSEMARY/ROSIE: Three! Oh, brother!

MAYANNAH: So this is the part where I officially thank you guys for braving the crazy streets and coming all the way here to be with me tonight.

LAYNA: Well, thanks for having us.

ROSEMARY/ROSIE: That goes double for me! Triple, even!

MAYANNAH: The rule is, whatever happens on the street tonight, it doesn't touch us. Up here we will have as much fun and be as happy as we can.

LAYNA: Okay—no pressure!

MAYANNAH: I have a feeling you two are going to be the best guests I ever had.

LAYNA: So all we have to do is eat, right?

MAYANNAH: And talk, really talk—no holding back, either of you—I didn't go through all this trouble to talk about the weather! At the end of dinner, there'll be a little monetary reward for you two, as we already discussed. Then everyone goes home. Easy, right?

LAYNA: Cash, check, or wire transfer?

ROSEMARY/ROSIE: Not to put the cart before the horse, but would it be kosher to get my hundred K in crisp, new five-dollar bills?

MAYANNAH: Make it to the end of dessert and you might get the keys to the whole, damn house!

ROSEMARY/ROSIE: Awesome!

LAYNA: Why wouldn't we make it to the end of dessert?

MAYANNAH: Okay, now—there's a lot to do. And I do it all myself. That's my rule.

(MAYANNAH *goes off to the kitchen.* LAYNA *and* ROSEMARY/ROSIE *regard each other warily, awkwardly.*)

LAYNA: So you don't know her either?

ROSEMARY/ROSIE: First time for me.

LAYNA: First time?

ROSEMARY/ROSIE: Technically, the second time, I guess. But it's the first time for me.

LAYNA: She seems nice. A little—uhm, odd—bit gloomy...

(MAYANNAH *appears, puts a platter of tostones on the table.*)

LAYNA: So! I, I changed outfits like eighteen times. It's been forever since I got asked out. Didn't know people still did that. Have dinner parties.

MAYANNAH: Because people are too afraid.

(ROSEMARY/ROSIE *is drawn to the food like the starving person she is.*)

ROSEMARY/ROSIE: Well, sure, all the curfews and tanks and—that looks yummy.

MAYANNAH: People were afraid before the curfews. Let's face it, people terrify. La Doña always tells me: nothing on earth can scare you like another human being. (*She goes off to the kitchen.*)

LAYNA: Thought I was the only one who thinks depressing shit like that.

ROSEMARY/ROSIE: You must think you're pretty special, then.

LAYNA: No, it's just—people worry me. You can't trust what they do or say. Like everyone around here is speaking their own language. And nobody tells the truth!

(MAYANNAH *appears, puts a steaming platter of rice and beans on the table, along with serving spoons, long knives, cleavers, long forks, skewers, and corkscrews.*)

MAYANNAH: Absolutely true!

LAYNA: Isn't that how we are? Always hiding from each other—so we never know what's really going on?

ROSEMARY/ROSIE: When do we stop the yakking and start the eating?

LAYNA: It's like we're geniuses at keeping the really good stuff—the far-too-easy-to-break stuff—buried so deep, no one can touch it. It makes me feel like I have to be a damn archeologist half the time, always digging below the surface of people, hoping, you know, for answers, some clarity, an actual, real glimpse at a person's, you know—soul.

MAYANNAH: An archeologist of personalities!

LAYNA: Yes! It's like a defense thing with me. So I don't get tricked or smashed or fucked, the way I look at people.

MAYANNAH: I noticed that about you. You keep staring at me and, uh, Rosie—

ROSEMARY/ROSIE: I'm sorry, but it gives me the heebies, all your staring, all your eyeballs googling at me.

LAYNA: I don't think of it as staring. I think of it as analyzing, like an X-ray.

ROSEMARY/ROSIE: "Layna", is it? Let me just say, Layna, that maybe you shouldn't dig too deep. Could hurt somebody.

MAYANNAH: Or scare yourself to death.

LAYNA: Good! It's called self-examination?

ROSEMARY/ROSIE: Well, I don't want anyone exploring me. Cracking my head open to look inside.

MAYANNAH: You won't look her in the eye. I noticed that about you.

ROSEMARY/ROSIE: Or listen to the words in my head. Some nights it's like the bloody B B C in there! Okay?!

LAYNA: Hey, back off a little!

MAYANNAH: There's some tension between you two and that's not what I'm paying for—

LAYNA: All I'm saying, okay, someone tells you to choose between being Socrates unsatisfied, or a pig satisfied. Obvious answer: Socrates.

ROSEMARY/ROSIE: Because pigs end up like this. On a plate.

MAYANNAH: It's not pig. In fact, it's not even remotely pig-like. *(She goes off to the kitchen.)*

LAYNA: Excuse me? What's she serving us?

ROSEMARY/ROSIE: So, Mayannah, how rich are you, anyway?

LAYNA: Look, if she's serving us people—not staying.

MAYANNAH: *(Off)* A lot fucking rich.

ROSEMARY/ROSIE: You never count it?

MAYANNAH: *(Off)* I don't like to think about the money.

ROSEMARY/ROSIE: If it was mine? I wouldn't think of anything else. It would be the air in my lungs and the man in my bed. And I would use it to get the hell out of this country but fast.

LAYNA: Amen to that.

MAYANNAH: *(Off)* Sometimes I think I should be living on the street, wallowing in filth, but my poor parents would not have wanted that for me...

ROSEMARY/ROSIE: Are they dead?

(MAYANNAH enters, with a huge steaming platter of meat covered in bright-red juices: organs, glands, legs, claws, muscles: bloody. She sets it carefully on the table.)

MAYANNAH: Dead as the meat on our table.

(LAYNA and ROSEMARY/ROSIE look at viscera that doesn't look like anything they've ever eaten before.)

LAYNA: Okay, you're going to think I'm—tell me it's not a person, okay?

MAYANNAH: You're too cute, Layna! A person!

ROSEMARY/ROSIE: I've never smelled anything like it. It has a hypnotic kinda scent.

MAYANNAH: Well, this is it, girls, tonight's meal. My parents bought these plates the first week they were married. The tostones and the arroz con gandules are the way we made them for generations. And the meat—very special. Special for tonight. For my two special guests. *(She pours three shots of rum, hands them out and raises her glass.)* Salud, dinero, y amor!

(LAYNA and ROSEMARY/ROSIE raise their glasses with less enthusiasm.)

LAYNA & ROSEMARY/ROSIE: To your health./ Cheers.

(The strong rum makes LAYNA and ROSEMARY/ROSIE cough, but has little effect on MAYANNAH.)

(MAYANNAH lights the long black candles, puts the napkins, glasses of water, loaves of bread, and other finishing touches on the table, and carefully watches LAYNA and ROSEMARY/ROSIE interact.)

MAYANNAH: So Layna, mi amor—didn't you just bring Socrates into the conversation?

LAYNA: Well, I don't know if what I said makes any sense—the self-examination thing?

ROSEMARY/ROSIE: Well, sure, you try to live up to these socially-imposed, impossible-to-live-up-to standards of beauty…

MAYANNAH: Wealth. Sex.

ROSEMARY/ROSIE: …sex, status, boob-size—it's enough to make you barking mad if you think about it too much.

LAYNA: Still, it's better than being naïve and satisfied with your un-examined self—leaving your heart open—getting your central nervous system chain-sawed by a man you thought actually loved you. Who actually gave two shits about you. But turns out all he wanted to do was fuck with your head!

MAYANNAH: Has someone had her heart broken?

LAYNA: It's just—I look around and it's like everyone's lost their souls. Did someone come and steal our souls when we were sleeping?

ROSEMARY/ROSIE: She didn't answer your question, Mayannah. Dodgy, that.

LAYNA: On the street, in bars, at home, every person out there—soulless, unreal. Like we're dead or dying or fake or faltering. Who could connect like that? Who could love like that? You want a relationship with a man? You might as well shadowbox with ghosts. You might as well make love to the wind.

ROSEMARY/ROSIE: Grim, sad world you live in, LAYNA.

LAYNA: Then you wonder if you yourself even exist!

ROSEMARY/ROSIE: Well, in Dublin we were busy surviving. We never obsessed about love and death like you Americans.

LAYNA: *(Skeptical)* Dublin…?

ROSEMARY/ROSIE: *(Impatient)* So? What are we waiting for?

(MAYANNAH *finishes her preparations.*)

MAYANNAH: Done! Girls—we're ready. Everyone. Sit. Now.

(MAYANNAH *sits,* ROSEMARY/ROSIE *and* LAYNA *on either side of her.* ROSEMARY/ROSIE *eagerly serves herself the arroz con gandules and shovels it in her mouth. Her first solid food in days.* LAYNA *munches on a tostone, wary and watchful.*)

ROSEMARY/ROSIE: I'll be buggered. I didn't know rice and beans could be so bloody luscious.

MAYANNAH: Layna—better not tell me you're not hungry. That's against the rules.

LAYNA: I'm working on it.

ROSEMARY/ROSIE: I can't believe you've done all this by yourself, Mayannah.

MAYANNAH: The whole staff got the night off. La Doña—she's the incredibly old woman who runs my life—El Doctor, El Cocinero, all of them. Every year, on this night, I make them leave me alone. I have to promise them I'll be okay with strangers.

ROSEMARY/ROSIE: Some day I'm going to have my own staff—and armed soldiers, like you, May'.

LAYNA: If you don't have a private army, you're not safe in this country.

MAYANNAH: The soldiers were La Doña's idea. They're supposed to keep us safe in case the food riots start again. Oh my God, those riots! "Eat the rich! Eat the rich!"

ROSEMARY/ROSIE: *(Quietly)* ...Eat the rich! Eat the rich!

MAYANNAH: But the soldiers don't make me feel any safer. The way they look at me. The dirty things they whisper. "I'd eat her! I'd let her fuck me!" *(Beat)* I haunt this place, I don't really live in it. I don't even see the staff much. I hear them. El Cocinero gossips about me. La Doña goes through my stuff looking for the weird drugs El Doctor gives me. I don't think that old witch is ever going to die. There's no way I'll ever be friends with these people.

ROSEMARY/ROSIE: Well, I don't think we're ever going to be happy or feel safe, period. At least I'm not. So to hell with it and pass that lovely plate of glands over there.

(MAYANNAH serves the meat.)

MAYANNAH: It's tiger. And it's amazing.

ROSEMARY/ROSIE & LAYNA: Did she/you say "tiger"!?

MAYANNAH: Can't wait for you guys to try it!

LAYNA: You never told us we were going to eat tiger.

ROSEMARY/ROSIE: We're having bloody tiger! Is it hard to get? Like is it U.S. Government Inspected?

MAYANNAH: El Cocinero gets it for me every year. Swears it's legal. Frankly, girls, I don't want to know.

LAYNA: Is it like eating a cat?

MAYANNAH: It's like nothing you ever had. It's unreal.

ROSEMARY/ROSIE: He looks beautifully unreal to me.

MAYANNAH: She. Female.

LAYNA: We're eating a girl tiger?

MAYANNAH: Oh, yes! Mommy-tiger was shot between the eyes and died in a splendid, red turbulence of blood. She left behind a whimpering little family wandering India, trying to remember what that bitch looked like.

LAYNA: That is fucked on so many levels.

MAYANNAH: No, there's justice to it. Animal justice. I may never eat greens again.

LAYNA: Think I'll just work on the nice tostones for now.

ROSEMARY/ROSIE: Light weight! *(She spears a slab of meat, puts it in her mouth and chews.)* Hmmm…Jesus, yeahhhhhh…!

MAYANNAH: It's inside you now!

ROSEMARY/ROSIE: I don't know if it's delicious because it's delicious, or it's delicious because it's endangered!

MAYANNAH: Filling all your cells!

ROSEMARY/ROSIE: I mean, how do you describe this taste?

MAYANNAH: I know what it tastes like. It tastes like sweet revenge.

LAYNA: O-kay…cryptic…

(MAYANNAH eats the tiger meat, relishing it.)

MAYANNAH: Do you girls ever ask yourselves—every time you put meat in your mouth, is the cliché true: are we really what we eat?

LAYNA: I—maybe—you mean—literally—?

MAYANNAH: When I eat this tiger, will I know what she knew? Will I be able to feel her mother's tongue licking her at birth? Will I know the thrill of the chase, the delicious heat of mating, and the sunsets in India?

LAYNA: Is that physically possible?

ROSEMARY/ROSIE: I am so totally going to India some day!

MAYANNAH: And if a tiger ate me, would she taste my personality and know my experiences? Would she know my childhood stories and dreams and every book I ever read? Would she love the same music I love? Would she love the same people? In every cell of this tiger, imagine: there's information, stories of the past, memories.

LAYNA: Jesus.

MAYANNAH: And what happens when a tiger gives birth? Is all the knowledge in the tiger's stomach passed down, genetically, from mother to child? Generation after generation? So, in a strange way, if you're eaten by a tiger do you basically live forever? *(Beat)* It's funny. So many changes happen in your life. Babies to adolescents to old age. Always going from one state of matter to another: like water goes from ice to steam. Especially when you die and you're buried. Flesh goes to dust, blood goes to soil, mind goes to air. But—if you're cremated? Does everything in your flesh and in your mind just float off with the smoke and ash? It makes you wonder, doesn't it: what's in the air right now?

ROSEMARY/ROSIE: Or who is.

MAYANNAH: Yes! Who!

LAYNA: Thanks for contributing that!

MAYANNAH: Whose life did you just suck into your lungs? How many times a day do you take in the evaporated dreams and remains of other people? And when you breathe in that smoke, carrying all that information and life—does it change you?

ROSEMARY/ROSIE: Could explain mood swings.

LAYNA: What? No! Mood swings are caused by chemical reactions in brain. I read that in a pretty good science mag—

MAYANNAH: My parents were cremated. I think of their final fire a lot. Their fingers burning. Eyes melting into their heads. Memories of me turning to smoke. Their life-stories floating in the air. Oh, how I wish I could've breathed them in! I wish I had a chance to feel their ashes and odors filling my lungs. God, please, just one last contact with the young lovers who conceived me...

(Hundreds of emergency sirens scream far below, sending waves of fear and foreboding through the women.)

MAYANNAH: No! Not tonight, Dios, por favor!

ROSEMARY/ROSIE: No, no, no...

*(*MAYANNAH *and Layna go to the window.)*

MAYANNAH: Thank God, they're not coming here...

LAYNA: I saw one of their sweeps in my neighborhood and it's sick how they grab people up and herd them in their vans.

MAYANNAH: There's never been a sweep down here. It must be something else. They're looking for someone.

LAYNA: Better not be one of you guys.

MAYANNAH: We can't worry about them tonight, Layna—I still have my soldiers. Let's sit down and eat. You haven't touched your tiger.

*(*MAYANNAH *leads* LAYNA *back to the table.* ROSEMARY/ ROSIE *is frozen, muttering.)*

ROSEMARY/ROSIE: ...no, no, no...

MAYANNAH: Rosie?

ROSEMARY/ROSIE: ...no, no, no...

(ROSEMARY/ROSIE *turns into* ROSEMARY/ROSALIND, *40s, aristocratic, arrogant, a slight mean-streak in her.)*

ROSEMARY/ROSALIND: —no, no, no, I'm sorry—but I'm starting to find this conversation a little horrendous. Count on Rosemary to get invited to the worst party in the city!

(LAYNA *and* MAYANNAH *look at* ROSEMARY/ROSALIND *surprised.)*

LAYNA: I thought you were having so much fun, Rosie.

ROSEMARY/ROSALIND: Rosalind. It's Rosalind.

LAYNA: Rosalind?

ROSEMARY/ROSALIND: Do I look like a Rosie?

LAYNA: Uh—yeah?

ROSEMARY/ROSALIND: Death, cremation, the police— why are you forcing me to think about things I don't want to think about? Don't you realize every word you say ricochets in my head—colliding with all the other crap—making things worse in there for everybody?

LAYNA: What's going on? Is she, like, the entertainment?

ROSEMARY/ROSALIND: Oh, wouldn't you like to know? You have no idea: the traffic, the chatter, the mind-boggling soap opera chaos in there!

MAYANNAH: It's like she put on someone else's eyes…

LAYNA: Okay, what is this? What are you trying to do to me? You into make-believe? Telling stories and lies?

ROSEMARY/ROSALIND: Oh why don't you just take your paranoia and shove it?

LAYNA: You're making me, oh, a tad nervous, okay? I like to have something firm under my feet when I—

ROSEMARY/ROSALIND: Maybe a little anecdote will help. One night, one of the kids Rosemary sits

for, Rosemary says to her, "It's past your bedtime,
Courtney, you have to be in bed," and Courtney
scrunches up her face and goes, "I know it's past my
bedtime but my brainpeople say I could stay up late
if I want." And that word gave Rosemary the chills.
Because she knows, down in the under-belly of her
heart, that that word—"brainpeople"—perfectly
captures this feeling she has about herself, this
nauseous, free-floating mental achy feeling, that she's
had since the politics started, since the knocks on her
door at midnight, this feeling she can't describe to
anyone but that pervades everything she does.

LAYNA: *(Getting it)* Oh my God.

ROSEMARY/ROSALIND: So, Mayannah, if a tiger ate
Rosemary would she inherit all the voices in her
head? Would she know all her brainpeople? Will she
remember all the screams? The darkness? And when
Rosemary eats her, this delicious tiger on this plate will
she enter her mind?

LAYNA: So which one is Rosemary?

ROSEMARY/ROSALIND: This is Rosemary: since the day
they let her stumble out of that hell in mental tatters,
the only job she can get is walking dogs. Taking care
of other people's babies. Anything low and servile,
involving lots of shit and crying you want to pay slave
wages for, she's your girl. That's the level of her self-
respect! That's how much they took away from her in
there! Your bathroom?

MAYANNAH: Left at the stuffed tiger.

(ROSEMARY/ROSALIND *exits to the offstage bathroom.*)

LAYNA: A total fucked-up, one-woman circus just
walked out of this room.

MAYANNAH: Yes. But don't you get it, Layna—she's so
porous…

LAYNA: I get it and it's not for me, thanks. Mayannah, it's been—wow. Truly. But, you know, between the sirens and the tiger meat and Sybil in the next room, you need to tell your driver to take me home.

MAYANNAH: Home? No!

LAYNA: I don't care about the curfew. Or how many points they're going to take from me.

MAYANNAH: But you haven't touched your food. That's part of the deal. At least have the tiger meat—

LAYNA: But I don't even know why I'm here. Maybe this was all a mistake. I don't care how much money you're giving me. I'll find another way to leave this country!

MAYANNAH: But do you know how much I paid those hunters to track down this tiger? The number of embassies I bribed to get the carcass into my kitchen?

LAYNA: Too bad but I don't seem to care.

MAYANNAH: But it's my anniversary dinner. The most important night of the year for me.

LAYNA: Look, it's hard enough for me to put myself in space when that space is mine. I don't go out, I work alone. So I don't have a lot of contact with other people. I really thought this might be fun, try out a few ideas, talk about Socrates!

MAYANNAH: But this is my yearly ritual: the meat, the blood, the strangers, and the crazy hope I invest.

LAYNA: But I don't even know what you're celebrating. You never told us.

MAYANNAH: It's hunger. Hunger is why we're here.

LAYNA: Oh, that's not creepy—or vague!

MAYANNAH: Mira, I'll double the offer. Two hundred thousand, cash, tonight, just sit down and eat your dinner.

LAYNA: Two hundred thousand? In cash?

MAYANNAH: This isn't going to be like the other years. I'm not going to let everything fall apart. I'm not going to scare everyone away. I don't care what it costs me.

LAYNA: You'd really make it two hundred K?

MAYANNAH: I can do everything better. Just let me start over. Music!

(MAYANNAH *goes to a record player, puts on an old bolero, starts to dance.*)

MAYANNAH: What kind of hostess am I? Letting everything get so morbid. Life's what's important tonight. Let's talk about life! Let's talk about love!

LAYNA: Let's talk about two hundred fucking thousand dollars!

(MAYANNAH *beckons to* LAYNA *and she goes to her. They slow-dance together.*)

LAYNA: Okay, life sounds good. Uh. Gee. So the parents are dead, huh?

MAYANNAH: Yes—but in life they were so in love, you couldn't be in the room with them when they got, you know, that way. In life my father was a big success in television.

LAYNA: Television? Really?

MAYANNAH: My Papi was seen and loved by millions. But that was before all the news programs had their balls cut off.

LAYNA: Seen? Your father was on the air?

MAYANNAH: Remember when they used to have international news? He did those. So I was told by La

Doña. You see, I have facts about my parents but no memories…

LAYNA: What time was your father on the air?

MAYANNAH: Twice every day.

LAYNA: At six and eleven?

MAYANNAH: At six and eleven! How did you know?

LAYNA: Now you're just fucking with me.

MAYANNAH: Were you a fan? But he died before you were born. For sure, if you saw him, though, he would've driven you crazy.

LAYNA: Stop saying things like that!

MAYANNAH: Made Mami so jealous! La Doña told me that, in Puerto Rico, my parents loved to take long walks along the beach together. They touched each other in shameless ways, in full view of the birds and joggers! La Doña says my parents were obsessed with tigers. She says they read Borges and Kipling to me every night, spoke about tigers in whispers, and understood them in some weird, amazing way. (Beat) She says my parents died together. In India. They had an accident. I was eight. That's something you don't forget. I just don't know why I forgot so many other things about them. You know how much money I'd pay to remember one thing about my parents that's all mine? That doesn't come to me pre-digested from a bunch of over-paid freaks who don't give a shit about me? Who never ask me if I was happy!

LAYNA: I'm sorry, Mayannah, that's sad, and you should see a qualified professional about that—

MAYANNAH: God, I love your hands, Layna. That was the first thing I noticed about you, the hands…

LAYNA: —but the fact that your father was on T V doing news at six and eleven freaks me out a bit because the man I was desperately in love with—

MAYANNAH: In photos of Mami, her hands are exactly yours. So soft. So dark! La Doña says Papi loved Mami's dark Taino skin. He called her "Mi India."

(LAYNA *pulls away from* MAYANNAH.)

LAYNA: Can you shut up about this?

MAYANNAH: I'm sorry, I talk about them so much because I didn't know them.

LAYNA: But "India!" That was my nickname growing up...

(ROSEMARY/ROSALIND *enters from the bathroom. She's turned into* ROSEMARY/ROXIE, *a happy-go-lucky agreeable hippy.*)

ROSEMARY/ROXIE: I really, really understand you, Mayannah, and I really, really support you.

LAYNA: Oh God, who's this one?

MAYANNAH: You do, Rosalind? Thank you!

ROSEMARY/ROXIE: Meet Roxie! And unlike some people who shall remain nameless, Roxie wants to hear all about your Mami.

MAYANNAH: Well, uhm, as I said, there was Taino Indian in her.

ROSEMARY/ROXIE: Then she must've been dark, like me!

LAYNA: Dark? Like you?

MAYANNAH: Papi's racist family didn't like her. So the day after they got married, they fled Puerto Rico for Los Angeles.

ROSEMARY/ROXIE: I love LA!

MAYANNAH: La Doña says it was hard for Mami at first, but Papi's pure green eyes reminded her of the Caribbean.

ROSEMARY/ROXIE: My eyes are green and pure!

LAYNA: Your eyes are green? That ain't green!

ROSEMARY/ROXIE: They're a little green, you bitchy lady person, so go fuck yourself even.

LAYNA: I got a better idea, why don't I go over there and kick your ass?

ROSEMARY/ROXIE: No! Do you know who you're talking to?

LAYNA: It's anyone's guess, Roxie, Rosie, Roseface, Rose Bud—!

(ROSEMARY/ROXIE *turns into* ROSEMARY/ROSE, *furious, intelligent, powerful.*)

ROSEMARY/ROSE: My name is Rose, and I gotta question for you. What makes you crazy? You got any idea, Layna? Sweet, sad Layna? Love makes you crazy. (*To* MAYANNAH) The death of a parent makes you crazy. (*Beat*) Sometimes an entire people go crazy. When you change the definition of simple words. When the abhorrent becomes familiar. When the absurd is routine. And no one seems to know the difference. Or if they know the difference, they don't talk about it, they're silent and that silence makes us crazy. (*Beat*) For Rosemary? It started with the housing project she was born into. The dogshit in the hallways, the airshafts where people dumped old trash, rum bottles, unwanted babies. It was the cockroaches that seemed to live in colonies under her eyelids. The young people—her childhood friends—who died of diseases reserved for the old. It was watching the cops burst into the living room to beat the shit out of her father. It was being driven insane by lottery numbers that never hit. It was the sick feeling that in the tenements and projects where she was raised—and where she'll probably die a lonely, miserable death that will never make the headlines—the rules are different than they are for all the rest of the world. *(Beat)* It was the day she rebelled against this silence. And she took to the streets. With her teacher and friends. And they shouted, "Eat the rich! Eat the rich!" —and the rich rolled out their private armies, clutching their wooden clubs and toxic gas. And they captured her. They put her in a cell…they put her in a cell…they put her in a…

(ROSEMARY/ROSE turns into ROSEMARY/ROZ, bookish, stuck-up.)

ROSEMARY/ROZ: …sell your books! Write what you know! So I write about the mind and it's wonderful adaptability. Ah, the mind! The more pressure, the more stress, instead of cracking like an egg, it gets more creative, more elastic and lucid and fertile, freer and freer to do whatever it needs to survive. I wrote three books on this! Prize-winners!

MAYANNAH: *(Confused)* Books?

(Before ROSEMARY/ROZ can respond, she turns into ROSEMARY/ROSA, unforgiving, hungry, feral, hyper-active.)

ROSEMARY/ROSA: Fuck books! They starve me! There's never any food when I'm around! *(She tears into the food, eats as fast as she can.)* It's their little power game. Hoarding the food, the light, the air. Rosie's the worst. Dublin slut! Always hogging the time and attention, like she's hot shit! But the others aren't much better. Rosalind is a compulsive narcissist. Roz, who you just met, ignores us because she has delusions of grandeur. P.S. her writing blows. Roseanne doesn't speak to Rose. The Teacher thinks we're idiots. And everyone's worried about Tom!

LAYNA: Who's Tom?

ROSEMARY/ROSA: I'm gonna save some food for Tom!
(Eating) What the others don't know is there's no
controlling a force of nature like me. They think I'm
something Rosemary made up in the dark, screaming,
lonely hole of her cell. But I'm as natural and real
and here as this awesomely tasty pile of flesh on my
plate. You see, I'm the custodian. The caretaker of our
little mental family. You try being that. Guardian and
witness to her life. Since the day of her release, I've
had to watch her scratch and scramble month after
month in some isolated shoebox in a building full of
freaks. Watching her sleep with the landlord for a
small discount on the rent. And I'm the only one—of
the hundreds of us—who bothers to talk to her. Who
whispers to her, night after night: "What happened
to your courage, girl? Your pride? You've got to get
back on your feet! The cause needs you! You could be a
hero!" Does she listen to me? No!

(MAYANNAH looks at the clearly upset LAYNA.)

MAYANNAH: We'll call it three hundred thousand.

ROSEMARY/ROSA: Yeah, she had it bad in there. It
was one continuous nightmare and thank God she's
forgotten it. The sensory depravation and beatings. The
serial rapes. But lots of others suffered worse and they
didn't crumble like she did. That's what pisses me off:
she broke. She lets the nightmares win time and time
and—

*(ROSEMARY/ROSA turns into ROSEMARY/TEACHER, a
benign, patient, older woman with a Southern accent.)*

ROSEMARY/TEACHER: Time is like a prison, children.
That's the lesson for all of you today. They torture the
person in the cell next to yours, and you hear Time
removing eyes and replacing them with marbles
covered with cataracts. Removing ears and replacing

them with shells stuffed with cotton. You hear knees being worn to the bone. Nerves plugged with mucus. Arthritis sprayed on the hands. Blood to the sex organs diverted to the thick, blue, intestine-shaped veins in the legs. Memories segregated into darker and deeper little rooms in the mind, as all the signs that tell you how to find those memories are covered in cobwebs and dust. The prisoner being tortured by Time in the cell next to yours doesn't scream. All you hear is the clock-like beat of torture instruments. And all you can do in your cell is wait for Time to finish with your neighbor and come for you. And you wait so long that on the day it comes to get you, you don't realize Time's already had its way with you—and you never even noticed. *(Beat)* What? What do you want to say? Don't you understand it's rude to interrupt? *(Beat)* Two minutes, Tom! You can come out and say—

(ROSEMARY/TEACHER *turns into* ROSEMARY/TOM, *a frightened little boy with a slight stutter.)*

ROSEMARY/TOM: Hi! Check it, I gotta t-talk fast 'cause they don't let me have a lot of t-time in Life! That's 'cause I'm such a prize fuck-up and I never get no chance to fix my shit, I mean, I just can't rewind my life and h-hope to do it better, can I?

MAYANNAH: Maybe you can.

ROSEMARY/TOM: So when I get out, I'm so lost, I can't do anything right and it m-makes me so sad and I can't stand myself no more—and I just wanna cut myself— bad.

(ROSEMARY/TOM *grabs one of the knives on the table and puts it to her arm.* LAYNA *and* MAYANNAH *rush to her.)*

MAYANNAH: Rosemary, don't!

LAYNA: Holy shit!

ROSEMARY/TOM: Hey, I know Rosemary's just like me. That's how come I just love her so much and I always fight the others, defending Rosemary—"g-give her a chance," I tell 'em. "Rosemary's really trying to get on with her life, you guys!" Man, Rosemary's so soft. Those pretty brown eyes. I kiss her when no one's looking. I'm not supposed to. She has dreams, and I watch them like movies, and they make me laugh. I don't get one thing—how come Rosemary knows Rosie and Rosa and all them others, but she don't know Tom. She don't know I'm here and how bad I wanna love her and heal her and marry her and start a family.

(ROSEMARY/TOM *puts the knife down and weeps.* MAYANNAH *quickly takes the knife.*)

(ROSEMARY/TEACHER *and* ROSEMARY/TOM *talk to each other.*)

ROSEMARY/TEACHER: Time to go to bed, Tom.

ROSEMARY/TOM: But I'm still hungry. And my brainpeople say I can stay up late if I want!

ROSEMARY/TEACHER: Nice try, but the lights are going out on you, Tom.

ROSEMARY/TOM: I hate the dark in here. All those voices scare me! Rosalind's so mean!

ROSEMARY/TEACHER: I love you, baby, don't cry.

ROSEMARY/TOM: Don't leave me alone, Teacher…

(ROSEMARY/TEACHER/TOM *turns into default-* ROSEMARY.)

ROSEMARY: …Oh my God…my head… (*She looks at* MAYANNAH *and* LAYNA *as if for the first time.*) …oh my God, where am I?

MAYANNAH: My house.

ROSEMARY: You. I remember you. You—invited me to your mansion, on some street only sheiks and king-pins can afford ... Saturday night.

MAYANNAH: Are you her...?

ROSEMARY: Does that mean it's Saturday right now?

MAYANNAH: Layna, I think this is the one I met that night—the one I invited. It's Rosemary.

LAYNA: Yay.

ROSEMARY: Oh my God, I've lost three whole days, haven't I? I've never lost three days in a row before. What have I been doing all this time?

MAYANNAH: We don't know, Rosemary, we just met you!

ROSEMARY: Oh God, this is bad. You know how much trouble I could have caused in three days? *(Checks her body out.)* No new scars, no bruises, nothing broken, okay, that's encouraging. Did I steal anything, break anything, sleep with anyone? Please don't judge me! You don't know me. You don't know what I go through. The black-outs—they were only minutes in the beginning—now they're days. That's a disaster! *(To herself)* Focus, Ro'. Don't spin out of control. First things first. You're not home. Deal with that. Find out where you are. Uhm, where are we?

MAYANNAH: Downtown. Flower Street.

ROSEMARY: That's miles from me. How did I get here?

MAYANNAH: I sent an armored limo to pick you up.

ROSEMARY: Dinner party. A hundred thousand bucks. You said you always ask two strangers. Are you the other one?

(Afraid, LAYNA doesn't answer.)

ROSEMARY: Have I offended you? Whatever I said to you before, I'm sorry—it wasn't me— *(Noticing the table)* Oh my God, did I eat this shit? Excuse me, but except for white meat, I'm a strict vegetarian!

LAYNA: Wait'll she finds out it's not pork.

ROSEMARY: This isn't funny. You just don't know what it's like for me. I wake up with ticket stubs in my pocket to places I never went to. On the street, women I don't know slap my face for sleeping with guys I never met. At home I open my diary and the words are in someone else's handwriting—the craziest shit you ever heard.

LAYNA: I bet that's true.

ROSEMARY: Oh my God, how many of them did you meet? All of them are imposters, no matter what they say. And each one, when they come out, they think they're the center, the essence of me. But they're not. There's only one, only me. I am Rosemary! *(She takes out a wallet full of pictures.)* That's me at eight. The projects where I grew up. My best friend Tom just before he died in police custody. My favorite teacher who taught me not to believe the lies they tell you. This girl I met in a bar called Dublin—she really loved to have a good time. Look: a drawing of me by Rosario. She draws me with horns and a tail because she hates me. They all hate me. They've tried to kill me. They've put rat poison in my food. You know how many times I've had my stomach pumped? They've cut my wrists. And I'm just a girl who wants a little normal happiness and no more drama, no more politics, and just maybe find someone to love me and make a family some day...believe me...

(ROSEMARY turns into ROSEMARY/ROSARIO, fiercely violent, malignant.)

ROSEMARY/ROSARIO: —when I say the one who says she's the real Rosemary is a liar. A killer. She's wanted for all those horrible murders in the projects. Mutilations. She's the one the police are looking for tonight. Don't trust her! HIDE THOSE KNIVES!!

(ROSEMARY/ROSARIO *turns into default* ROSEMARY.)

ROSEMARY: —God, what are you looking at? What's wrong? What just happened? You don't believe me, do you? You think I'm one of them telling you stories. You don't believe I'm really here—

ROSEMARY/ROSIE: —You're not here!

ROSEMARY/ROXIE: —You're not here!

ROSEMARY/ROSE: —You're not here!

ROSEMARY/ROSARIO: —YOU WERE NEVER HERE!

(ROSEMARY *turns into* ROSEMARY/ROSALIE, *a woman so old and slow, she barely moves or breathes.*)

ROSEMARY/ROSALIE: My.

MAYANNAH: Hello?

LAYNA: She's dead, right?

(MAYANNAH *touches* ROSEMARY/ROSALIE'*s forehead, and pulls her hand away.*)

MAYANNAH: Ay! Hot!

LAYNA: *(Putting knives away)* What's going on with her?

MAYANNAH: It's like she over-heated…she shut down.

LAYNA: I'm ready to shut down.

ROSEMARY/ROSALIE: Mind.

MAYANNAH: She's going to be fine. I think she's just resting.

LAYNA: Are you sure we don't need your doctor? Maybe he's got a spare straight jacket?

MAYANNAH: Poor thing. You wanted to know what the soul is like? This one's in shreds because of what they did to her...

LAYNA: How can you be so calm? You know what you brought into your house?

MAYANNAH: I do.

LAYNA: And that's cool with you?

MAYANNAH: It is.

LAYNA: So is that why you picked her? Because she's a village?

MAYANNAH: I picked her for her lovely eyes.

LAYNA: Them why, out of this endless army of screwed up people that night in front of the bar, why did you have to pick me?

MAYANNAH: I told you.

LAYNA: Yeah, my hands. "Lovely eyes, lovely hands." That explains the whole thing.

MAYANNAH: Some more rum?

LAYNA: I mean, for all I know you and Rosemary are working together to play some wicked sick game on me.

MAYANNAH: Why would we do that?

ROSEMARY/ROSALIE: Has.

LAYNA: Who needs a reason to be cruel anymore? It's sport. It's fun. It's: let's see how much we can get away with.

MAYANNAH: Layna, that's a little paranoid—

LAYNA: You're the one with the fucking army! And the naked Jesuses!

MAYANNAH: But I've given you no reason to—

LAYNA: Don't you think this happens to me all the time? That I'm victim to little bouts of mental cruelty a dozen times a day? Don't you think I feel the creepy little war going on out there between the weak and the strong?

MAYANNAH: But we can make something with the three of us that's real and healthy—

LAYNA: Healthy? I haven't slept in days. I'm so alone, I'm free-falling. People and the words they say don't connect. I don't recognize the world I was born into. Everyone's got secrets but no one's got privacy. And soon as it gets dark, the soldiers crawl out like vampires and make things worse.

MAYANNAH: But with me and Rosemary, in this house, you don't have to be alone.

LAYNA: But something in me was stolen. I'm beyond alone. I'm less than myself.

MAYANNAH: But don't you feel potential between us? To be more than friends? More than lovers?

LAYNA: Mayannah, I came here for money. Not to be friends. Money. Please, give me the money so I can go.

MAYANNAH: I can't.

LAYNA: Look, I really need to get out of this country. To live in some village somewhere. Not just because of what this country's become, which is bad enough, heart-breaking enough. I need to go so I can forget him. To be where everything doesn't remind me of how stupid I've been…

MAYANNAH: Say it with me: men are mierda.

LAYNA: When he turned on me he didn't just take himself away, he took pieces of all my important organs, slices of my memories, half my prayers. I was channel-surfing the first time I saw Miguel…

MAYANNAH: My father's name!

LAYNA: It was a sea of faces. So many of those T V
faces are plastic, like the opposite of attractive. But
there he was suddenly. I couldn't take my eyes off
him. He wasn't plastic or perfect but that's what made
him perfect. I started seeing him right away. At six,
I'd turn on the T V and get in bed. At first I'd close my
eyes and just listened to him. I wouldn't give myself
the pleasure of looking at his face. Just to heighten the
suspense and joy. Then I'd open my eyes to watch his
mouth form those words, those lips around those orb-
shaped vowels, and I'd get so horny. By the time I took
care of business, his broadcast was over and I turned
him off until eleven, and it would start all over again.

ROSEMARY/ROSALIE: Been.

LAYNA: Why did everything have to turn to shit? All
I wanted was to look at him, listen to him. There was
all this endless stuff between us. It was the only time
I understood what "infinity" meant. Like there was
an infinite number of choices between us, an infinite
number of ways to be happy. And for one sweet
month, I thought I was pregnant! I had dreams of a
daughter with wild, dark hair, like yours. But she was
just a dream.

MAYANNAH: A dream.

LAYNA: Then one night at six, I turned on the T V and
he didn't say anything. He just sat there, staring at me.
I didn't know what to do, so I hit the side of the T V—
and he "woke up" and started his broadcast. Okay,
weird. But then he did the same thing at eleven—
except this time he had a scary, annoyed reaction when
I hit the TV. Same thing happened the next day! I got
so freaked, I changed to another channel! I mean, I
can't be in a relationship, even if the sex is great, if I'm
scared of the other person, you know? I'm not crazy

for thinking that, right? Then I woke up one morning.
It was that first week of martial law. And my T V was
already on! And there he was. Just staring at me. And
I lost it. I started screaming: "Leave me alone! You're
too crazy for me! It's over between us!" I was walking
up and down, foaming at the mouth, and that's when
I saw his eyes following me. Well, I unplugged the T V
and threw it out the window.

ROSEMARY/ROSALIE: Ruined.

LAYNA: A few nights later I was in the only
government-approved bar in my neighborhood,
drowning my sorrows, and I didn't notice the T V. It
was eleven. I was the only woman. The streets were
quiet except for the armored vehicles. The place was
full of cigarette smoke—and tension. Because no one
knew what was going to happen. When the news came
on, I thought they were going to show that woman
who set herself on fire in front of the Supreme Court
to protest the canceled election and the arrest and
torture of the dissidents—but, no—it was him. With
a really nasty look on his face. I'm screaming: "You
can't hurt me anymore, motherfucker!" He smirked!
The sound was off but the captions were on. So I
started reading. You know what I read? The fucker
was reading my diary! On the air! All the men in the
bar got, like, riveted to my sordid life story. To all the
ways love turns to shit. To all the creative abuse men
have turned into art-forms. To all the tricks I used just
to survive. My face turned white from dread, then red
from anger. And the men standing around me, who
were learning all the dark secrets of a single woman's
mind, they were hooked. Some took notes. Some texted
their buddies. All laughed at my dumb, pathetic life.
When they saw my face change colors, they figured
out it was me they were reading about. All their eyes
locked on me. This piece of nervous meat who had

the balls to think she knew how a man's great mind
worked. Those eyes started to strip me, Mayannah. To
pull off my clothes, then my skin. Then all the inner
goo, down to the electricity in my nerves, to my soul,
which they tried to see with their X-ray eyes, reducing
me to nothing, to air, to moisture, to nothing. When
they knew everything they needed to know about
me, I didn't need to exist. *(Beat)* I left the bar crying
and grabbed a streetlamp so I wouldn't fall over and
that's when a stranger with morbid eyes and black hair
walked up to me and knew I'd be too weak and lonely
to say no to her beauty, her wealth, and her invitation
to dinner on Saturday night...

ROSEMARY/ROSALIE: By.

LAYNA: I used to look to a lover to reflect myself
back to me, to describe reality to me: I'd know about
my soul that way; I'd have some idea of my own
intelligence and value because of the dented mirrors
my lover held up, and I'd look into them and search
for the truth and try to understand what my soul was
made of. This man taught me that all these mirrors lie,
Mayannah. They lie.

ROSEMARY/ROSALIE: Poverty.

LAYNA: Now, when I'm in bed, and think about love
and what it does to my heart, I can feel my heart
changing shape. First it's a pyramid, then it's round
and hard like a fist, then soft and gooey like a giant
amoeba—never valentine-shaped or pretty or pink.
And it always feels way too big for my body. And all
I want is to take my big, freakish heart and get out of
this country and go into the world and find a love so
good and real, it will make my heart change into a true
valentine shape. But my heart always seems about to
collapse under its own weight and I'm sure I'm going

to die from its crazy hunger and its unbearable ability to feel. Does that make any sense?

MAYANNAH: Si, mi amor, si.

(MAYANNAH *goes off.*)

ROSEMARY/ROSALIE: My.

(MAYANNAH *comes back with a black leather bag.*)

LAYNA: What's that?

MAYANNAH: Enough money to get you out of this country forever. What happens to your heart after that, Layna, I don't know.

(MAYANNAH *hands the money to* LAYNA.)

LAYNA: Wow—this is mine? I don't have to do anything for it?

MAYANNAH: You've gone through enough. Just take the money and go home. I'll watch over her—them— until they're okay to go.

LAYNA: I'm really done?

MAYANNAH: If you want to go now, I'll call the driver.

ROSEMARY/ROSALIE: Mind.

LAYNA: Someone who keeps their word. That's new in my life. I guess maybe I was wrong about you.

MAYANNAH: I'm sorry we never got to be friends.

LAYNA: I'm sorry I was so high-maintenance tonight.

ROSEMARY/ROSALIE: Has.

(MAYANNAH *starts to clear the table, blowing out the black candles, etc.*)

LAYNA: This totally ruins your plan for tonight, doesn't it? This whole thing you do every year. I mean, what did you expect me and Rosemary to do?

MAYANNAH: It doesn't matter now. It was stupid…

LAYNA: Well, I think it's cool you wanted me and Rosemary to be your friends. I know what it's like to live without any love. I hope that changes for you. Maybe you'll meet someone nice sometime?

MAYANNAH: *(The meat)* I'll have to throw this all out...

LAYNA: Have you ever loved anyone like I did? Crazy like that?

MAYANNAH: My mind has been ....

ROSEMARY/ROSALIE: Been.

MAYANNAH: There are forms of love I just don't know and don't think I'll ever know.

LAYNA: I know all the shitty forms. Like I have a PhD in it.

MAYANNAH: If I want love, well, este, it's a good thing I'm filthy rich.

LAYNA: You pay for men?

ROSEMARY/ROSALIE: Ruined.

MAYANNAH: Men, boys, women, groups on tour. El Doctor checks them out. Says it's good for me to do it as much as I can. But I have rules. I never have the same person more than once. No names. And I'm not supposed to enjoy it, Layna. Sometimes I put nails in my bed. I once made love to a man in a coffin. I had sex with a woman on her dying day. I felt her final breath on my cheek—and I came.

LAYNA: Just when I'm starting to like you...

MAYANNAH: I can only have sex that takes me far from all this, where I can smell the dirt in my grave and feel the rough chill of my tombstone.

ROSEMARY/ROSALIE: By.

MAYANNAH: Where do you go—even if it's just in your dreams? You and your love?

LAYNA: I see us on the beach. The waves make, like, liquid sucking sounds. And we touch each other in broad daylight right in front of...

LAYNA & MAYANNAH: ...the birds and joggers.

LAYNA: The trouble is, he made me think the only true, good, free, perfect love is the love you imagine.

MAYANNAH: Because he broke something in you.

LAYNA: Is that why I miss him so much?

MAYANNAH: It's not him you miss. What you miss is yourself, unbroken.

ROSEMARY/ROSALIE: Poverty.

LAYNA: I do. You should've seen me as a little girl. I was so tough. So cool.

MAYANNAH: I was that kind of girl too.

LAYNA: Maybe we could've been friends. You're a nice person.

MAYANNAH: You think so?

LAYNA: Well, a little too gothic for your own good, and maybe I would redecorate a little...

ROSEMARY/ROSALIE: My.

MAYANNAH: That night, in front of the bar, on the one day in the year I go out, and I love it because it feels like freedom, and that feeling scares me in a good way, I saw so many people. I rejected them all. Except for Rosemary who had these haunted eyes I couldn't forget. And there was something in your hands, Layna. Like I knew them before.

LAYNA: Like from another life?

MAYANNAH: Hands that put me to bed. Hands that held copies of Borges and Kipling. Hands that worked so hard for my future.

LAYNA: A better life?

MAYANNAH: A better life. Yes.

LAYNA: How do you find that? A better life? A completely new way to live? Do you have to do like Rosemary and be so many people maybe one of them will survive and be happy?

ROSEMARY/ROSALIE: Mind.

MAYANNAH: Maybe we could do that. If we can be friends. Maybe it's not too late to find a new way to live. Really live, you know?

LAYNA: Out of this country?

MAYANNAH: Away from the staff and the soldiers—

LAYNA: —and the past—

MAYANNAH: —and the animal meat. What do you think? You and me and all the Rosemaries!

LAYNA: Could get crowded.

MAYANNAH: We'll live in a big house, in a cool, obscure country. We'll go topless all day and cook big meals together!

LAYNA: No endangered species!

MAYANNAH: You could find love. Rosemary could find peace and wholeness. I could wear another color besides black. I could travel to India and see tigers in person. I'll finally finish this madness. And we could start right now. We don't have to wait for anyone's permission. I'm a goddamn grown woman. And I have money.

ROSEMARY/ROSALIE: Has.

MAYANNAH: I could sell these rocks—or use them like dollar bills. I can bribe the driver. We can flirt with the soldiers.

LAYNA: I know how to flirt.

MAYANNAH: We'll buy new I Ds on the black market and start our lives tonight, Layna. Yes?

LAYNA: Yes.

MAYANNAH: Yes!

ROSEMARY/ROSALIE: Been.

(MAYANNAH *takes out her cellphone.*)

(*Another series of eerie police, fire, and emergency sirens— closer this time, louder.*)

(MAYANNAH *listens, immobile.*)

LAYNA: May'…?

ROSEMARY/ROSALIE: Ruined.

(LAYNA *goes to the window looks out.*)

LAYNA: It's okay, they're going somewhere else.

(MAYANNAH *puts the phone down.*)

MAYANNAH: What do I think I'm doing?

LAYNA: It's okay—we can go.

MAYANNAH: I didn't go the first time … I can't go now…

LAYNA: I can call the driver if you can't.

MAYANNAH: No. I can't do it. I can't go.

LAYNA: With all that money, we can do anything—

MAYANNAH: Fuck the money—!

(MAYANNAH *tears at her earrings, necklaces, and bracelets and throws them on the floor.* LAYNA *grabs her and makes her stop.*)

LAYNA: What's wrong with you? Why can't you get out of this morgue? What the fuck is keeping you here?

ROSEMARY/ROSALIE: By.

MAYANNAH: Can you tell me…why would God curse a child, Layna?

LAYNA: Did God curse a child? Is that what happened to you?

ROSEMARY/ROSALIE: Poverty.

MAYANNAH: I can't look out a window or an open door without wanting to throw up.

LAYNA: C'mon, stop it.

MAYANNAH: Every room I look into, it's the same room. The same thing happens there.

LAYNA: What room?

MAYANNAH: I don't want to go in there again—

LAYNA: Where is the room?

MAYANNAH: I said I don't want to go in there! I don't want to see it anymore!

LAYNA: If you don't go back into that room, you're never going to leave it. Is that what you want? To be stuck? So next year you can go out and find two more pathetic losers to freak out? And the year after? When does all this end, May'?

ROSEMARY/ROSALIE: My.

MAYANNAH: I don't know if I can tell you—

LAYNA: If not us, then who? That staff you never talk to? The soldiers? The police who tortured poor Rosemary? Your dead mother and father? They can't hear you. They can't take care of you. I can hear you, though. I can.

(Beat)

MAYANNAH: It's a church. It's a church, Layna!

ROSEMARY/ROSALIE: Mind.

MAYANNAH: It's a church.

LAYNA: I'm getting that it's a church.

MAYANNAH: An old church in Puerto Rico.

LAYNA: Make me see it. Take me there.

MAYANNAH: The three of us are in the church.

ROSEMARY/ROSALIE: Has.

MAYANNAH: It's my first time in this old church. They were married here. I'm so nervous, I need to pee. I'm so little, I have to look up to see everything. Mami was here. Papi here.

ROSEMARY/ROSALIE: Been.

MAYANNAH: Holding hands.

LAYNA: Holding hands.

MAYANNAH: Everyone's looking at us. That's because my Papi drives women crazy. Young women whisper his name as he walks by—

LAYNA: Miguel!

MAYANNAH: They say it with such heat. La India doesn't like it.

LAYNA: But you love it, don't you?

MAYANNAH: Yes. I'm proud. I have the best Papi. But I see him only on Sundays and on T V. When he reads the international news. I always kiss the T V when he's on. And he always smiles when I do it. He once read my poem on T V.

LAYNA: It all sounds so good, so perfect.

ROSEMARY/ROSALIE: Ruined.

MAYANNAH: It's the day of my First Communion. The three of us hold hands up the aisle. Ay, the smells. Camellias, "Old Spice", "Paradise". My new black shoes are tight. I'm in a long white dress Mami made by hand for me. My hair done all special. The floor creaks. The air is humid, old. In the pews, poor people, on their knees, pray to la Virgen for lottery numbers to hit, for pregnancies to end well, for husbands to stop cheating—they beg and beg for a million secular miracles. Then I see him.

ROSEMARY/ROSALIE: By.

MAYANNAH: He's…almost as big as Papi. Almost… naked. I'm scared. I want to pull back. Then I see the blood! In front of me is a young man impaled on an upside-down sword, nailed into space. And—he's sweating, he's breathing. He's still alive. And he knows that I know. His dark eyes move—his mouth opens—he tries to say something to me. I scream: "Help him! Get him down from there! My parents don't know what's wrong with me. And I don't know why everyone keeps walking past this poor, handsome young man—those strong, long muscles. Those thin, hard hips—those dark eyes full of old music—his soft, fleshy mouth. And I'm the only one who can see him the way he really is. His eyes beg me to wipe his bloody face and soothe his young, mighty heart, to take him home, feed him rice and beans, put my fingers in his wounds—and eat his sorrow. I run out of the church. He haunts me all day. Even after my parents laugh at me for thinking that the huge wood crucifix in the back of the church is real. They tell all their friends what a boba I am for ruining my First Communion. That night we have dinner. Lots of meat and butter. It's pouring rain. I'm talking about a book report. My parents are excited because they're going to India to shoot pictures of tigers in the wild. This would be the first trip they'll take without me—and I'm hopping mad. And I can't stop thinking of the crucifix because I know it's a bad omen, and I try to warn them not to go to India without me and they just think I'm being

childish and that's the last time I see them alive. I'm
not in India to protect them and they don't come back.

ROSEMARY/ROSALIE: Poverty.

MAYANNAH: I wait by the window. Months pass. I
scream for my parents, for answers. Then I just stop
screaming. *(Beat)* La Dona forges some documents
and takes control of my parents' fortune. She sets up a
corporation to raise me. The house is full of sad-eyed,
silent staff members, dressing me, feeding me, listening
to me rant and rave, trying to relate to this stunned,
eight-year-old orphan. Nobody kisses me. When I
start demanding some affection, La Dona tells me my
parents were eaten by tigers. Only parts of their bodies
were recovered. Those few bones were cremated. That
ends it for me.

ROSEMARY/ROSALIE: My mind.

MAYANNAH: So every year I celebrate the anniversary
of our last night together as a family by paying two
complete strangers to have dinner with me, and
serving them tiger meat.

LAYNA: But, Mayannah, you can't say that was your
fault—

MAYANNAH: Yes! If I had just convinced them to take
me—

LAYNA: That's why you're torturing yourself? You
were just a child.

MAYANNAH: And every year, I do everything I can to
recreate that final meal: the dishes, the rum, the tiger
meat. But year after year, no matter how perfectly I
planned it, the miracle never happened. Then I realized
it can't be just any tiger. There was only one and I had
to find her.

ROSEMARY/ROSALIE: Has been.

MAYANNAH: That's why I was so sure this year would be different. This year El Cocinero told me: "We found her! The daughter of the tiger who ate your mother and father! This is her!"

LAYNA: This one's the daughter? That's who we're eating tonight?

ROSEMARY/ROSALIE: Ruined by.

MAYANNAH: Look at her. She's magnificent. Such a waste. That's why I asked you: are we really what we eat? And can we ever really know, Layna, what mysteries are passed down from mother to daughter?

LAYNA: Or who is.

MAYANNAH: Yes, who.

LAYNA: That's why we're here. To eat the past.

ROSEMARY/ROSALIE: Poverty. My.

MAYANNAH: I figured something out when the Rosemaries exploded and you talked about your love. All I wanted was to take back what the world stole from me. But now I think...this meal, this night, doesn't belong just to me. This is also her night—and yours.

LAYNA: Mine?

MAYANNAH: I can give you all the money I have. What will change, Layna? Really change. Your heart? Your place in this dirty food chain we live in? I think tonight, Layna, it's possible, just possible, I don't know, but I think I can give you something more than the money you crave. I can give you, and poor Rosemary...

ROSEMARY/ROSALIE: Mind has been.

(MAYANNAH *pulls out* LAYNA's *chair at the table, inviting her to sit.*)

MAYANNAH: ...a whole new life.

(LAYNA *takes a breath, sits at her place at the table, picks up her fork.*)

LAYNA: A whole new life. (*She stabs the tiger meat, puts it in her mouth and eats…an unexpected smile.*) Wow, it is good. Like chicken only not!

ROSEMARY/ROSALIE: Ruined by poverty.

(LAYNA *hungrily eats the tiger meat.*)

(MAYANNAH *looks at her as if expecting something to happen.*)

(*After a few moments,* LAYNA *stops, confused.*)

LAYNA: I don't feel anything. What was I supposed to feel?

MAYANNAH: I don't know exactly…

(LAYNA *gets up from the table. Goes to* MAYANNAH, *hugs and kisses her.*)

LAYNA: It didn't work. I'm sorry. Maybe it's me. Maybe I don't have the magic.

ROSEMARY/ROSALIE: My—mind—has—been— ruined—by—poverty…

LAYNA: Aaaaaand she's back.

(ROSEMARY/ROSALIE *becomes* ROSEMARY/MIGUEL, *a middle-aged, aristocratic Puerto Rican man, and stares at* LAYNA.)

ROSEMARY/MIGUEL: La India? Mi amor, is that you?

(LAYNA *doesn't know how to respond. She looks at* MAYANNAH.)

LAYNA: Is that—him?

MAYANNAH: Ay Dios mio.

ROSEMARY/MIGUEL: You look frightened, my India!

LAYNA: Is she—? Is he—?

ROSEMARY/MIGUEL: That's your nickname, isn't it?

LAYNA: Yes, but—

ROSEMARY/MIGUEL: What would you like to do? How do we start to trust each other?

LAYNA: I don't know what to do, Mayanna.

ROSEMARY/MIGUEL: May I suggest...

(Feeling weak, LAYNA takes off her glasses.)

LAYNA: And I really feel weird...

ROSEMARY/MIGUEL: ...that we do something...

LAYNA: *(Weaker)* I should go...

ROSEMARY/MIGUEL: ...like this?

(ROSEMARY/MIGUEL goes to LAYNA and gently kisses her.)

(The kiss seems to send a jolt through LAYNA's body.)

(As ROSEMARY/MIGUEL kisses LAYNA, MAYANNAH gasps—not from surprise, but because it looks so familiar.)

LAYNA: Oh my God...

(ROSEMARY/MIGUEL goes to the necklace MAYANNAH had ripped off her body, picks it up, and puts on around Layna's neck. Takes down her hair.)

(A struggle in LAYNA's mind and body as she becoming LAYNA/INDIA, a young aristocratic Puerto Rican woman.)

ROSEMARY/MIGUEL: I ask again: how do we start?

LAYNA/INDIA: Do we take a walk, Miguel?

MAYANNAH: A walk would be perfect.

ROSEMARY/MIGUEL: A walk would be perfect!

MAYANNAH: Along a body of water.

LAYNA/INDIA: Along a body of water.

ROSEMARY/MIGUEL: Something deep, ancient, and not too polluted.

LAYNA/INDIA: Reminding us that we're shallow, young, and a little dirty.

ROSEMARY/MIGUEL: No words for a long time.

LAYNA/INDIA: Words would ruin it.

ROSEMARY/MIGUEL: We let the tide and the moon have their conversation.

LAYNA/INDIA: They talk about love and attraction.

ROSEMARY/MIGUEL: They talk about gravity and moisture.

LAYNA/INDIA: Would I stop during our walk? Would I stop in your path?

ROSEMARY/MIGUEL: And face me. Block my way.

LAYNA/INDIA: My two strong legs slightly apart. My mouth open.

ROSEMARY/MIGUEL: The moon and the tide stop talking. They watch us. Anticipation is killing them.

LAYNA/INDIA: I spend a long time looking at your face. Planning my move.

ROSEMARY/MIGUEL: My hands sweat.

LAYNA/INDIA: Do I forget how I was raised? Good Catholic girl? A good family? One of the best in Puerto Rico! A reputation as long as history itself!

ROSEMARY/MIGUEL: Anticipation is killing me!

LAYNA/INDIA: Do I forget all that and simply let your hand come down inside my legs, Miguel?

ROSEMARY/MIGUEL: Not a bad way to start the day!

LAYNA/INDIA: I want to stop you, but I can't. Everything I've been taught about men—it's all true! Pigs, all of you!

ROSEMARY/MIGUEL: Gracias! Then?

LAYNA/INDIA: I'm afraid I'll be seen. Not by God—but by the staff my parents employ to spy on me! Their princess! Their prisoner!

ROSEMARY/MIGUEL: Then we go to eat. We talk about the future.

LAYNA/INDIA: I examine every word you say. I try to sift the lies from the half-truths.

ROSEMARY/MIGUEL: I'm all about the truth.

LAYNA/INDIA: It takes more than one dinner.

ROSEMARY/MIGUEL: It takes days, then months.

LAYNA/INDIA: And I learn how to love you.

ROSEMARY/MIGUEL: And I learn all of you.

LAYNA/INDIA: But your family doesn't trust you me. They're so white they think they're from Spain.

ROSEMARY/MIGUEL: But your green eyes and dark Taino skin devastate me. And we marry.

LAYNA/INDIA: In an old church.

ROSEMARY/MIGUEL: With an ageless, life-sized crucifix of wood.

LAYNA/INDIA: Then. Slowly. Easily. With visions of angels in our heads.

ROSEMARY/MIGUEL: And in our dreams, night after night...

LAYNA/INDIA: We make a child.

ROSEMARY/MIGUEL: We make a child.

LAYNA/INDIA: We make a child.

ROSEMARY/MIGUEL: The child is beautiful, with long wild hair and dark eyes and she's the third, final, and most perfect part of this little world we've created. She saves us from each other, from the wild animals that stalk our imaginations. She's our purpose, our compass. Something in her that seems to keep us alert through all the morbid dangers of daily life...like a good luck charm.

(LAYNA/INDIA *and* ROSEMARY/MIGUEL *turn to* MAYANNAH.)

LAYNA/INDIA: Are you hungry, mi'ja?

(The sound of rain as it pelts the big windows.)

MAYANNAH: No.

ROSEMARY/MIGUEL: Why not?

MAYANNAH: 'Cuz.

ROSEMARY/MIGUEL: Oh, I know why...

(ROSEMARY/MIGUEL *mimes the crucifixion and laughs.)*

LAYNA/INDIA: Don't tease her again, Miguel.

ROSEMARY/MIGUEL: When did I say anything—?

MAYANNAH: You're laughing.

LAYNA/INDIA: She's sensitive.

ROSEMARY/MIGUEL: Ay Dios, when did I say a word—?

LAYNA/INDIA: If she starts crying again...

ROSEMARY/MIGUEL: She's not going to cry. Are you, Mayannah?

MAYANNAH: No. Depends.

ROSEMARY/MIGUEL: You made a little mistake. There's not enough light in that stupid church. And, when you think about it, they don't have to make it look so real. So bloody. Sadistic Catholic bastards!

(LAYNA/INDIA *laughs, crosses herself.)*

LAYNA/INDIA: Ay Dios, Miguel, watch what you say in front of the child!

ROSEMARY/MIGUEL: Right, mi cielo?

MAYANNAH: Si. Catholic bastards.

LAYNA/INDIA: I hope you're pleased with yourself!

MAYANNAH: Do I have to eat?

LAYNA/INDIA: Of course you have to eat. This is the last night we're going to eat together for three weeks.

MAYANNAH: Jesus killed my appetite.

ROSEMARY/MIGUEL: Ven aqui!

LAYNA/INDIA: You're going to spoil our last dinner...

ROSEMARY/MIGUEL: Pobrecita. Que te vengas aqui, carajo!

(MAYANNAH *approaches* ROSEMARY/MIGUEL *tentatively.*)

MAYANNAH: Not funny, Papi.

ROSEMARY/MIGUEL: I know; my sweet angel of an angel; I know...

(ROSEMARY/MIGUEL *and* MAYANNAH *hold each other a long moment.*)

MAYANNAH: Okay, I'm hungry now.

LAYNA/INDIA: How the hell do you do that?

ROSEMARY/MIGUEL: Now sit down now and stop being foolish, boba.

MAYANNAH: Yes, Papi. You're the boba! (*She sits.*)

(LAYNA/INDIA *serves food.*)

ROSEMARY/MIGUEL: This lechon smells like heaven itself...

MAYANNAH: We shouldn't eat meat.

ROSEMARY/MIGUEL: Pity the poor vegetarian, I say!

(LAYNA/INDIA *pours rum and lights black candles.*)

(MAYANNAH *runs to the record player and turns it on, excited. A Bolero plays.*)

LAYNA/INDIA: What are you going to do while we're gone besides miss us?

MAYANNAH: Book report.

ROSEMARY/MIGUEL: On?

MAYANNAH: Tigers!

ROSEMARY/MIGUEL: Ah!

MAYANNAH: I said it a million times!

LAYNA/INDIA: You don't need to be sarcastic, young lady.

MAYANNAH: But he never remembers! Ugh!

ROSEMARY/MIGUEL: My memory. Worthless! Shoot me in the head, por Dios!

LAYNA/INDIA: I can't tell you how excited I am about this trip. We need this trip.

(ROSEMARY/MIGUEL *and* LAYNA/INDIA *hold each other and dance close.* ROSEMARY/MIGUEL *smiles at* MAYANNAH.)

ROSEMARY/MIGUEL: Oye. We'll take pictures for you. We'll have many, many pictures of tigers for your book report.

MAYANNAH: It's not fair. Why can't you take me? I can help. I'm not a baby. The Jesus in church—scared me. His eyes did. It's bad luck if you see Jesus still alive. I read that in the stupid Bible! If you go without me, it's bad. I feel it. And you can't leave me with La Doña. She's a big, fat liar! Please? What if I never see you again? Mami, Papi, will you please take me to India with you to see the tigers?

(ROSEMARY/MIGUEL *and* LAYNA/INDIA *look at each other.*)

ROSEMARY/MIGUEL: What do you think?

LAYNA/INDIA: We made our plans.

ROSEMARY/MIGUEL: Can't we change our plans?

LAYNA/INDIA: Can we change what's already done?

ROSEMARY/MIGUEL: She's been good.

LAYNA/INDIA: Can we change what's meant to be?

ROSEMARY/MIGUEL: We can change whatever we want to change, mi India.

LAYNA/INDIA: She's been so very good, that's true.

ROSEMARY/MIGUEL: She has been perfect.

MAYANNAH: Is that yes?

(ROSEMARY/MIGUEL *and* LAYNA/INDIA *stop dancing.*)

ROSEMARY/MIGUEL: Si, mi cielo. The answer, tonight— is always—was always—and will forever be always—

MAYANNAH: ...Yes!

(ROSEMARY/MIGUEL, LAYNA/INDIA *sit at the table.*)

(MAYANNAH *hugs them.*)

MAYANNAH: ...Yes, I'm going.

(MAYANNAH *looks around—at her resurrected parents, at the world that's completely changed.*)

MAYANNAH: I'm going.

(MAYANNAH *pours herself a shot of rum, takes a sip, and coughs.* LAYNA/INDIA *and* ROSEMARY/MIGUEL *laugh at her and begin to eat.*)

(*The family eats together, lively, animated, laughing...as lights go down on them, the bolero gets louder, and police sirens fill the air—then black out.*)

END OF PLAY

www.ingramcontent.com/pod-product-compliance
Lightning Source LLC
Chambersburg PA
CBHW070030110426
42741CB00035B/2704